L'ANGLAIS POUR LES ENFANTS

I SPEAK ENGLISH TOO! 1

ISBN: 978-1-914911-11-8

www.zigzagenglish.co.uk

ZIGZAG ENGLISH

OUR BOOKS FOR CHILDREN

www.zigzagenglish.co.uk

Our bilingual books for young children. *Funny stories in simple, useful everyday English, with colour photos.*
English with Tony -1- Tony moves house
English with Tony -2- Tony is happy
English with Tony -3- Tony's Christmas
English with Tony -4- Tony's holiday
My Best Friend

Our coursebook for child beginners *(age 7 to 11)*
English for Children - 1st Coursebook (Essential vocabulary and grammar for beginners)

Our series of dialogue books for beginners *(for beginners aged 7 - 11). With word lists, comprehension questions, speaking tasks and more.*
I Speak English Too! - 1
I Speak English Too! - 2

Our series of reading and comprehension books for beginners *(for beginners aged 7 - 11). With word lists, comprehension questions and more.*
Read English with Zigzag - 1
Read English with Zigzag - 2
Read English with Zigzag - 3
Read English with Zigzag 1, 2 and 3
        Audiobook - Books 1 + 2 (Audible)

The Learn English Activity Book for Children *(A1 - A2, elementary). (Recommended for children in early secondary school.)*

Our series of reading and comprehension books for children at elementary level *(recommended for ages 10 - 13). With word lists, comprehension and discussion questions and lots of language activities.*
Read English with Ben - 1
Read English with Ben - 2
Read English with Ben – 3

Our series of reading and discussion books (with writing tasks) for children at secondary school, A2 - B1
I Live in a Castle – Book 1 – The Choice
I Live in a Castle – Book 2 – The New Me

The Speak English, Read English, Write English Activity Books – *3 books from A1 to B2, for older children and adults.*

Our non-fiction book with language activities
Learn English with Fun Facts! – A2 – B2

English Dialogues for Secondary School – for ages 11 to 17, A2 – B2

OUR BOOKS FOR ADULTS

Our 3 Grammar books with grammar-focused dialogues
Learn English Grammar through Conversation – A1, A2 and B1

Our Dialogue books for adults (with vocabulary lists and comprehension questions)
50 very Easy Everyday English Dialogues (A2)
50 Easy Everyday English Dialogues (A2 - B1)
50 Intermediate Everyday English Dialogues (B1 - B2)
50 more Intermediate Everyday English Dialogues (B1 - B2)
40 Advanced Everyday English Dialogues (B2 – C1)
40 Intermediate Business English Dialogues (B1 - B2)
40 Advanced Business English Dialogues (B2 - C1)

Our activity books for adults and older children
The Speak English, Read English, Write English Activity Books – 3 books, for A1 - A2, A2 - B1 and B1 – B2.

Our non-fiction book with language activities
Learn English with Fun Facts! – A2 – B2

Contents

Les objectifs de cette série de livres:

1. Donner à votre enfant la confiance nécessaire pour lire et parler anglais.

2. Enseigner à votre enfant, de manière ludique, des mots et des phrases clés, qui seront ensuite utilisés pour l'aider à élargir son utilisation de l'anglais.

Notre méthode pour enseigner l'anglais aux enfants:

1. Ces livres ont été écrits par une enseignante d'anglais qualifiée et expérimentée. Ils ont été testés par des enfants d'âge primaire qui apprenaient l'anglais à partir de zéro.

2. Si vous parlez un peu d'anglais, vous pouvez utiliser ces livres pour aider votre enfant. Vous n'avez pas à vous inquiéter de faire des erreurs - vous pouvez simplement lire les phrases du livre. Mais si vous le souhaitez, vous pouvez aller plus loin en utilisant les dialogues pour avoir de nouvelles conversations avec votre enfant.

3. Les dialogues sont bien sûr parfaits pour les frères et sœurs aussi.

4. Les dialogues commencent par les bases et ajoutent ensuite des mots et des phrases pour développer l'anglais de votre enfant. Il peut apprendre davantage grâce à des questions de compréhension, des "Remplir les Blancs" et des "Recherches de Mots".

5. En 23 dialogues, votre enfant passera de "Hello. What's your name?" à "Can you buy Christmas presents there? I want to buy presents for my family."

6. Et il sera alors prêt à passer au livre 2!

Comment utiliser ce livre:

1. Lisez le <u>dialogue A</u> avec votre enfant.

2. Regardez ensemble <u>la liste de vocabulaire</u> et aidez votre enfant avec les nouveaux mots.

3. Changez de rôles et lisez à nouveau le dialogue.

4. Encouragez votre enfant à faire l'exercice. L'exercice "Fill the Gaps" peut être fait sans se référer aux phrases originales - c'est un défi amusant. Ou, plus facilement, vous pouvez demander à votre enfant de regarder les phrases manquantes - elles se trouvent en bas de l'exercice - et de choisir les bonnes. Les réponses aux questions de compréhension des dialogues 2, 4, 6, 8 et 10 se trouvent à la fin du livre.

5. Lisez le dialogue B. Changez de rôles et relisez-le.

6. Posez à votre enfant les questions à *C: What about you?*

7. Si vous le souhaitez, vous pouvez essayer une conversation avec votre enfant en utilisant le langage des dialogues A et B, ainsi que le langage des dialogues précédents. Vous pouvez bien sûr introduire de nouveaux mots et de nouvelles phrases. Selon nous, c'est la manière la plus efficace d'enseigner l'anglais à un enfant. Vous aiderez votre enfant à élargir son utilisation de l'anglais jour après jour.

Quoi d'autre? Et après?

1. Au fur et à mesure que l'anglais de votre enfant s'améliore, essayez d'introduire des livres de lecture et des livres audio en anglais facile. Pourquoi ne pas essayer notre série de livres pour enfants de niveau débutant: **Read English with Zigzag**? C'est l'histoire d'un chat, d'un chien, d'un frère et d'une sœur. C'est drôle! Il y a beaucoup d'images! Les livres comprennent également des listes de vocabulaire anglais / français, des questions de compréhension et des activités linguistiques. Il y a aussi un **livre audio**.

2. Passez au **I Speak English Too! - 2** pour aider votre enfant à passer au niveau suivant.

3. C'est passionnant de voir son enfant faire des progrès rapides dans une nouvelle langue. Bonne lecture, et amusez-vous bien!

LESSON 1

1A: Hello! Where do you live?

Anna: Hello.

Katie: Hello. What's your name?

Anna: My name's Anna. What's your name?

Katie: I'm Katie. How are you?

Anna: I'm fine. How are you?

Katie: I'm okay, thank you. How old are you?

Anna: I'm ten. How old are you?

Katie: I'm nine. You're big! I'm small. My sister is big.

Anna: What's your sister's name and how old is she?

Katie: Her name is Jessica. She's eleven.

Anna: Where do you live?

Katie: I live in **the UK**. I live in **Cambridge**. Where do you live?

Anna: I live in Paris, in France. Paris is big. Is Cambridge small?

Katie: It's not **very** small, but it's not very big. Do you like Paris?

Anna: Yes, I do. I like it. It's **nice**. Goodbye, Katie.

Katie: Bye, Anna.

Vocabulary
- the UK   le Royaume-Uni
- Cambridge – a city in the south east of England
                                 une ville du sud-est de l'Angleterre
- very   très
- nice   agréable

1A: Fill the gaps

Anna: Hello.

Katie:

Anna: My name's Anna. What's your name?

Katie:

Anna: I'm fine. How are you?

Katie:

Anna: I'm ten. How old are you?

Katie:

Anna: What's your sister's name and how old is she?

Katie:

Anna: Where do you live?

Katie:

Anna: I live in Paris, in France. Paris is big. Is Cambridge small?

Katie:

Anna: Yes, I do. I like it. It's nice. Goodbye, Katie.

Katie:

1. *I live in the UK. I live in Cambridge. Where do you live?*
2. *Bye, Anna.*
3. *I'm Katie. How are you?*
4. *It's not very small, but it's not very big. Do you like Paris?*
5. *Her name is Jessica. She's eleven.*
6. *I'm okay, thank you. How old are you?*
7. *Hello. What's your name?*
8. *I'm nine. You're big! I'm small. My sister is big.*

  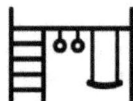

1B

Sam: Hello!

Jack: Hello. I'm Jack. What's your name?

Sam: My name's Sam and my **big brother's** name is Andrew.

Jack: Are you okay?

Sam: Yes, I'm fine. How are you?

Jack: I'm okay, thanks.

Sam: Are you eleven?

Jack: No, I'm **not**. I'm not eleven, I'm ten. How old are you? You're big!

Sam: I'm eleven. I live in Cambridge. Do you live in Cambridge too?

Jack: Yes, I do. I live in Cambridge too. Cambridge is small.

Sam: Yes, it's **quite** small.

Jack: Bye, Sam.

Sam: Goodbye, Jack!

Vocabulary
- big brother   grand frère
- not   pas
- quite   assez

1C: What about you?

1. *What's your name?*
2. *How are you?*
3. *Where do you live?*

LESSON 2

2A: My mum's English and my dad's French

Anna: Hello Katie. How are you **today**?

Katie: Hi Anna. I'm fine, thanks. Is that your mum?

Anna: Yes, it is.

Katie: What's your mum's name?

Anna: Her name's Claire.

Katie: Is she nice?

Anna: Yes, she's very nice.

Katie: Is your mum French?

Anna: No, she's not. My dad's French, but my mum's not. She's English.

Katie: Does your dad **speak** English?

Anna: No, he doesn't. My mum speaks English and French. My dad speaks French, but he doesn't speak English.

Katie: My mum and dad are English. They speak English. I speak English and **a little bit** of French.

Anna: Do you really speak French? That's great!

Vocabulary
- today   aujourd'hui
- to speak   parler
- a little bit   un peu

2A: Find the right answer

1. Is Anna's mum French?
   - a. No, she's not, she's English.
   - b. Yes, she is. She's French.
   - c. No, she's not, she's American.

2. Does Anna's mum speak French?
   - a. No, she doesn't, she speaks English.
   - b. Yes, she does, she speaks French and English.
   - c. She speaks a little bit of French.

2B

Jack: Hi, Sam.

Sam: Hi!

Jack: Are you okay?

Sam: Yes, I'm fine, thanks.

Jack: Is that boy your brother?

Sam: Yes, he's my big brother. His name's Andrew.

Jack: How old is he?

Sam: He's quite big. He's twelve.

Jack: Do you like him?

Sam: Yes, I do. I quite like him. He's okay. Do you have a brother?

Jack: No, I don't. But I have a little sister. She's very small. She's five.

Sam: Do you like her?

Jack: No, I don't. I don't like her. She's too small. She's **boring**.

Vocabulary
- boring   ennuyeux

2C What about you?

1. *What's your mum's name?*
2. *Is your dad English?*
3. *Does your mum speak English?*

LESSON 3

3A: I like it

Katie: What do you like, Anna? Do you like **ice cream**?

Anna: Yes, I do. I like ice cream **a lot**.

Katie: I like ice cream too. I like ice cream and chocolate.

Anna: I like ice cream, I like chocolate, and I like chocolate ice cream!

Katie: What don't you like?

Anna: I don't like **peas**. I **really** don't like them!

Katie: Do you like your **house**?

Anna: Yes, I do. My house is very nice. It's quite big.

Katie: I like my bedroom. It's quite small, but I like it.

Anna: What colour is your bedroom?

Katie: It's green.

Anna: Green is a nice colour. Is it your **favourite** colour?

Katie: No, it's not. I like green, but my favourite colour is red.

Anna: I like green and red too. My favourite colour is orange. My bedroom is blue, but my **bed** is orange. I love it!

Vocabulary

- ice cream   glace
- a lot   beaucoup
- peas   pois
- really   vraiment
- house   maison
- favourite   favori
- bed   lit

3A: Fill the gaps

Katie: What do you like, Anna? Do you like ice cream?

Anna:

Katie: I like ice cream too. I like ice cream and chocolate.

Anna: I like ice cream, I like chocolate, and I like chocolate ice cream!

Katie: What don't you like?

Anna:

Katie:

Anna: Yes, I do. My house is very nice. It's quite big.

Katie: I like my bedroom. It's quite small, but I like it.

Anna:

Katie: It's green.

Anna: Green is a nice colour. Is it your favourite colour?

Katie:

Anna: I like green and red too. My favourite colour is orange. My bedroom is blue, but my bed is orange. I love it!

1. *Do you like your house?*
2. *No, it's not. I like green, but my favourite colour is red.*
3. *What colour is your bedroom?*
4. *I don't like peas. I really don't like them!*
5. *Yes, I do. I like ice cream a lot.*

3B

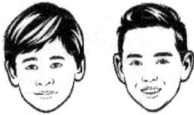

Sam: Do you have a dog, Jack?

Jack: No, I don't. **But** I have a very nice cat.

Sam: What colour is your cat? Is it black and white?

Jack: No, it's not. It's brown and white. Do you have a cat **too**?

Sam: No, I don't have a cat. My dad doesn't like cats. But I have a dog.

Jack: Do you have a big dog or a small dog?

Sam: It's not very big. It's quite small.

Jack: What colour is it?

Sam: It's black.

Jack: What's its name?

Sam: Its name is Fluffy.

Jack: Fluffy is a nice name. I like dogs. I **want** a dog.

Sam: You want a dog and I want a cat!

Vocabulary
- but   mais
- too   aussi
- to want   vouloir

3C What about you?

1. *What do you like?*
2. *What don't you like?*
3. *Do you have a cat?*
4. *Do you want a dog?*

LESSON 4

4A: Friends

Katie: **How many** friends do you have, Anna?

Anna: I have quite a lot of friends. I have six or seven friends. Do you have a lot of friends?

Katie: No, I don't. I have three friends.

Anna: Do you have a **best friend**?

Katie: Yes, I do. My best friend's name is Ben.

Anna: I have a best friend too. Her name's Sara. She's ten.

Katie: What does she **look like**?

Anna: She's very **tall**. She's quite **thin**.

Katie: Ben is **short**. He's a bit **fat**. He's a very nice boy. I like him a lot.

Anna: How many brothers and **sisters** does he have?

Katie: He has two brothers and two sisters. He has a big **family**.

Anna: Sara has a small family. She has no brothers or sisters. But she has a lot of friends.

Katie: Does she speak English?

Anna: She speaks a little bit of English. And a lot of French!

Vocabulary

- how many — combien de
- best friend — meilleur ami
- to look like — ressembler à
- tall — grand
- thin — mince
- short — petit
- fat — gros
- sister — sœur
- family — famille

4A: Find the right answer

1. What is Anna's best friend's name?
   a. It's Ben
   b. Her best friend's name is Sara.
   c. She doesn't have a best friend.

2. Does Sara speak English?
   a. Yes, she speaks a lot of English.
   b. No, she doesn't speak English.

      c. Yes, she speaks a little bit of English.
3. How many friends does Anna have?
      a. She has three friends.
      b. She doesn't have a lot of friends.
      c. She has quite a lot of friends.

4. How many brothers and sisters does Ben have?
      a. He has a big family. He has three brothers and two sisters.
      b. He has no brothers or sisters. His family's small.
      c. He has four brothers and sisters.

5. Is Sara short and thin?
      a. Yes, she is. She's short and thin.
      b. No, she's not. She's short and fat.
      c. She's thin, but she's not short.

4B

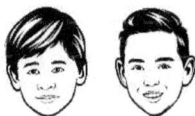

Sam: Do you like my big brother, Jack?

Jack: Your brother Andrew? Yes, I do. He's nice. I like him. He's very tall, isn't he?

Sam: Yes, he's quite tall. What does your little sister look like?

Jack: She's not tall. She's very short. She's quite fat. She has **long** brown hair. She has big brown eyes.
Sam: Andrew has short **fair** hair and blue eyes.

Jack: You have short fair hair too. But you don't have blue eyes. You have brown eyes, don't you?

Sam: Yes, I do. What's your sister's favourite colour?

Jack: It's yellow. She likes yellow a lot. What's Andrew's favourite colour?

Sam: I don't know.

Vocabulary
- fair   clair

4C What about you?

1. *How many friends do you have?*
2. *Do you have a best friend?*
3. *What does your friend look like?*
4. *What's your friend's favourite colour?*

LESSON 5

5A: Sara's house

Katie: **Where** does your best friend live, Anna?

Anna: My friend Sara?

Katie: Yes. Does she live in Paris?

Anna: Yes, she does. She lives **near** my house.

Katie: What's her house like? Does she live in a big house?

Anna: No, she doesn't. Her house isn't very big, because she has a small family. But it's quite nice. It has a **beautiful garden**.

Katie: How many **bedrooms** does her house have?

Anna: It has two bedrooms. Does your house have two bedrooms too?

Katie: No, there are three bedrooms in my house. One for me, one for my sister and one for my parents.

Anna: What's your **living room** like?

Katie: We have a **lovely** living room. It has a big blue sofa and an **enormous** television. The living room is my favourite room.

Vocabulary
- where   où
- near   près de
- beautiful   beau
- garden   jardin
- bedroom   chambre à coucher
- living room   salon
- lovely   beau
- enormous   énorme

5A: Fill the gaps

Katie: Where does your best friend live, Anna?

Anna: My friend Sara?

Katie: Yes. Does she live in Paris?

Anna:

Katie: What's her house like? Does she live in a big house?

Anna:

Katie: How many bedrooms does her house have?

Anna:

Katie: No, there are three bedrooms in my house. One for me, one for my sister and one for my parents.

Anna: What's your living room like?

Katie:

1. *No, she doesn't. Her house isn't very big, because she has a small family. But it's quite nice. It has a beautiful garden.*
2. *We have a lovely living room. It has a big blue sofa and an enormous television. The living room is my favourite room.*
3. *It has two bedrooms. Does your house have two bedrooms too?*
4. *Yes, she does. She lives near my house.*

5B

Sam: Where do you live, Jack? Is your house near here? Is it near the park?

Jack: No, it's not. It's near the big Tesco's **supermarket**.

Sam: I live quite near the park. Not **far** from the **cinema**.

Jack: What's your house like?

Sam: I live in a **flat**. It's very small. It has two bedrooms – one for my parents and one for me and my brother.
Jack: Does it have a nice living room?

Sam: No, not really. The living room is **tiny**.

Jack: Do you have a garden?

Sam: No, we don't. But we live near the park, so that's okay.

Vocabulary

- supermarket   supermarché
- far   loin
- cinema   cinéma
- flat   appartement
- tiny   minuscule

5C What about you?

1. *Where does your friend live?*
2. *What's your friend's house like?*
3. *How many bedrooms does your house have?*
4. *Does it have a nice living room?*

LESSON 6

6A: Two pets

Katie: Do you like animals, Anna?

Anna: Yes, **of course** I do. I love animals.

Katie: Do you have a **pet**?

Anna: Yes, I have two pets. I have a **rabbit** and a **hamster**.

Katie: Why do you have a rabbit AND a hamster?

Anna: Because one pet isn't **enough**. I don't want a rabbit OR a hamster – I want **both**!

Katie: Do your parents like your two pets?

Anna: No, not really. But my friends like them.

Katie: Hamsters are okay; but I don't like rabbits.

Anna: Why not? Why don't you like them?

Katie: Because they **bite**!

Vocabulary

• of course	bien sûr
• pet	animal de compagnie
• rabbit	lapin
• enough	assez
• both	les deux
• to bite	mordre

6A: Find the right answer

1. Does Anna hate animals?
   a. No, she doesn't. She quite likes animals.
   b. She doesn't hate them but she doesn't like them.
   c. Of course not! She loves animals!

2. How many pets does Anna have?
   a. She has one pet. It's a cat.
   b. She has two pets – a rabbit and a hamster.
   c. She doesn't have any pets.

3. Who likes Anna's pets?
    a. Her parents like them.
    b. Her friends like them.
    c. Katie likes them.

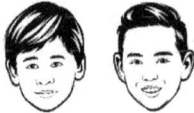

6B

Jack: I really want a dog, Sam.

Sam: Don't you have a cat?

Jack: Yes, I do. I like my cat, but I want a dog too.

Sam: Dogs are nice, but they're very **messy**.

Jack: Cats aren't messy. But they're a bit boring.

Sam: Cats are beautiful. I want a cat, but my dad doesn't want one.

Jack: Does your mum want a cat?

Sam: Yes, she does. She likes cats a lot. But my dad really doesn't like them.

Jack: Does your brother like cats **or** dogs?

Sam: He likes **snakes**.

Jack: Snakes? I **hate** snakes!

Vocabulary

- messy   sale
- or   ou
- snake   serpent
- to hate   détester

C What about you?

1. *Do you have a pet?*
2. *Do you like animals?*
3. *Does your mum like snakes?*

Word Search 1

```
W K V V G A G Y P T Y W F L V
I G M A Q F A X E T E T M J C
H T A I V O R U T I N Y Q B H
D U P Y B N D U S Q E G U O O
M G C L O V E L Y E A G I R C
P E W U S E N E F R R R T I O
R I M Z H R Y S H O R T E N L
K C H K I Y A T I P L M W G A
N H M R N K E A D A V M A W T
Q Y C Y G T A U L R R W J Y E
S W F W W L I V R E X F Z E Y
H Z D D Y B L U K N Y U B R L
F A V O U R I T E T B C P Q I
O R I V H Z B S A S Y A X Y C
V T V H O Y H N Y M H B U T W
```

- I love , but I don't like ice cream.
- Your mum and dad are tall, but my **p_re_t_** are **s_or_**.
- I don't like your house. It's too small – it's **t_ny**! But your **g_rd_n** is **l_ve_y**!
- My best friend has a **_er_** nice **p_t**. It's a cat.
- What's your **fa_our_te** pet? Dogs. Hamsters are **q_it_** nice too, but rabbits are **b_r_ng**.
- Do you live **n_ar** the cinema?

LESSON 7

7A: What time is it?

Katie: What time is it in Paris, Anna?

Anna: It's nine o'clock.

Katie: Nine o'clock? It's eight o'clock **here**. It's **early**.

Anna: Do you have school today?

Katie: No, I don't. Are you at school?

Anna: Yes, I am.

Katie: What time do you **go to school**?

Anna: I **get up** at seven o'clock. I go to school at eight o'clock. I **start** school at half past eight.

Katie: I start school at a quarter to nine. I get up at eight o'clock, and **run** to school! Do you **walk** to school?

Anna: Yes, I walk to school. It's near my house.

Vocabulary
- here   ici
- early   tôt

- to go to school   aller à l'école
- to get up   se lever
- to start   commencer
- to run   courir
- to walk   aller à pied

7A: Fill the gaps

Katie: What time is it in Paris, Anna?

Anna:

Katie: Nine o'clock? It's eight o'clock here. It's early.

Anna:

Katie: No, I don't. Are you at school?

Anna:

Katie: What time do you go to school?

Anna:

Katie: I start school at a quarter to nine. I get up at eight o'clock, and run to school! Do you walk to school?

Anna:

1. Yes, I am.
2. Do you have school today?
3. Yes, I walk to school. It's near my house.
4. I get up at seven o'clock. I go to school at eight o'clock. I start school at half past eight.
5. It's nine o'clock.

<u>7B</u>

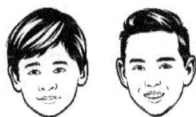

Sam: Do you like school, Jack?

Jack: No, not really. School starts too early. It starts at ten to nine.

Sam: That *is* early. My school starts at a quarter past nine.

Jack: What time is your **lunch break**?

Sam: We have lunch at twenty to one.

Jack: And **when** do you go **home**?

Sam: At a quarter to four.

Jack: That's quite **late**. We go home at five past three.

Sam: When do you **do your homework**?

Jack: I don't have a lot of homework. My mum **drives** me to school, and I do my homework in the **car**!

Vocabulary
- lunch break   pause de midi
- when   quand
- home   à la maison
- late   tard
- to do homework   faire ses devoirs
- to drive   conduire
- car   voiture

7C What about you?

1. *What time is it?*
2. *What time do you go to school?*
3. *What time do you have lunch?*
4. *Do you walk or run to school?*
5. *Do you have a lot of homework?*

LESSON 8

8A: It's cold

Anna: Is it cold in Cambridge? It's not cold in Paris. It's quite **warm**.

Katie: It's cold here. My house is quite cold. But my school is too **hot**.

Anna: Where are you? Are you at school?

Katie: No. I'm in my bedroom.

Anna: I'm in my bedroom too.

Katie: Is your sister **there**?

Anna: No, she's in the **kitchen**. But my friend Sara is **here**.

Katie: Where are your pets?

Anna: My rabbit's here, in my bedroom. But my hamster is in my sister's bedroom.

Katie: Does your sister like your hamster?

Anna: Yes, she loves my hamster. She wants my hamster to live in her bedroom. But she doesn't really like my rabbit.

Katie: Why not? Does your rabbit bite?

Anna: **Maybe** a little bit.

Vocabulary

• cold	froid
• warm	assez chaud
• hot	chaud
• there	là
• kitchen	cuisine
• here	ici
• maybe	peut-être

8A: Find the answers

1. Is it cold in Paris?
    a. Yes, it is. It's quite cold.
    b. No, it's not. It's quite warm.
    c. Yes, it is. It's cold and rainy.

2. Where's Sara?
    a. She's at home.
    b. She's in Cambridge.
    c. She's in Anna's bedroom.

3. Why doesn't Anna's sister like her rabbit?
    a. Because it bites.
    b. Because it's boring.
    c. Because it's not a hamster.

8B

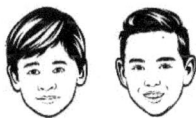

Sam: It's really cold today.

Jack: It's **always** cold in Cambridge.

Sam: No, it's not; not always.

Jack: When it's not cold, it **rains**.

Sam: No; **sometimes** it's hot and **sunny**.

Jack: I'm cold. I'm very cold.

Sam: Do you want to go home?

Jack: Yes, I do. Do you want to **come** to my house?

Sam: Is your house cold too?

Jack: No, it's not. It's really warm in my house.

Sam: Great! **Let's go!**

Vocabulary
- always   toujours
- to rain   pleuvoir
- sometimes   parfois
- sunny   ensoleillé
- to come   venir
- let's go   allons-y

8C What about you?

1. *Is it cold today? Or is it hot and sunny?*
2. *Where are you?*

LESSON 9

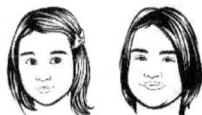

9A: What's your school like?

Anna: What's your school like, Katie? Is it nice?

Katie: It's okay. I quite like it. Do you like your school?

Anna: Yes, I do. It's a very good school.

Katie: How big is the school?

Anna: It's big. There are **about** five **hundred children**.

Katie: How many boys and how many girls are there?

Anna: I don't know. But there are fifteen girls and ten boys in my class.

Katie: That's a lot of girls.

Anna: Yes. Do you have a lot of girls in your class?

Katie: No. **Half** my class are boys.

Anna: Is your best friend in your class?

Katie: No. He doesn't go to my school. He goes to a **different** school.

Anna: Oh, that's bad **luck**.

Vocabulary
- about   environ
- hundred   cent
- child/ren   enfant/s
- half   moitié
- different   différent
- luck   chance

9A: Fill the gaps

Anna:

Katie: It's okay. I quite like it. Do you like your school?

Anna:

Katie: How big is the school?

Anna:

Katie: How many boys and how many girls are there?

Anna:

Katie: That's a lot of girls.

Anna:

Katie: No. Half my class are boys.

Anna:

Katie: No. He doesn't go to my school. He goes to a different school.

Anna:

1. *I don't know. But there are fifteen girls and ten boys in my class.*
2. *Oh, that's bad luck.*
3. *Yes, I do. It's a very good school.*
4. *Is your best friend in your class?*
5. *It's big. There are about five hundred children.*
6. *Yes. Do you have a lot of girls in your class?*
7. *What's your school like, Katie? Is it nice?*

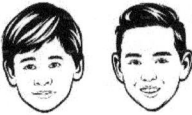

9B

Sam: What are the teachers like at your school?

Jack: They're not bad. We have **some** very **good teachers.**

Sam: **What's your teacher called**?

Jack: She's called Mrs Brown. Her **husband works** at the school too.

Sam: What does he do? Is he a teacher too?

Jack: No. He's a **cook**. He cooks our school **lunches**.

Sam: Is he a good cook?

Jack: **I think so**. We have a lot of **fish and chips**. I love fish and chips!

Sam: I don't have school lunches. I **take** sandwiches to school.

Jack: Don't you think sandwiches are boring?

Sam: Yes, they are a bit boring. I have **cheese** sandwiches **every day**!

Vocabulary

• some good teachers	de bons professeurs
• what's…called?	comment s'appelle…?
• husband	mari
• to work	travailler
• cook	cuisinier
• lunch	déjeuner
• I think so	je pense que oui
• fish and chips	poisson et frites
• to take	prendre
• cheese	fromage
• every day	tous les jours

9C What about you?

1. *How big is your school?*
2. *How many children are there in your class?*
3. *What's your teacher called?*
4. *Do you take sandwiches to school?*

LESSON 10

10A: Clothes

Anna: Does your school have a uniform, Katie?

Katie: Yes, of course it does. Don't **all** schools have a school uniform?

Anna: No. My school doesn't. Lots of schools in France don't.

Katie: Really? **Lucky** you! I hate my school uniform.

Anna: **Why** do you hate it? What is your uniform?

Katie: Girls and boys all wear black **trousers**, a white **shirt** and a purple **top**.

Anna: That sounds okay. What's wrong with that?

Katie: Some girls don't like trousers. They want to wear **skirts**.

Anna: So do the boys like the uniform?

Katie: No, not really. Lots of boys don't like purple.

Anna: Why not? I love purple. I **often** wear purple tops to school.

Katie: **Seriously**?!

Vocabulary

- all — tout
- lucky — chanceux
- why — pourquoi
- trousers — pantalon
- shirt — chemise
- top — haut / pull
- skirt — jupe
- often — souvent
- seriously — sérieusement

10B

Sam: Do you like **shopping**, Jack?

Jack: Yes, I love shopping. I like **buying new clothes** with my mum.

Sam: **How often** do you buy new clothes?

Jack: Quite often. Maybe **once a month**.

Sam: I like new clothes too. But my mum says they're too **expensive**.

Jack: Some clothes shops are **cheap**. And buying **online** is cheap too.

Sam: I really want some new **trainers**. But the ones I like are very expensive.

Jack: Maybe **wait** till **Christmas**?

Sam: What do you want for Christmas?

Jack: I want a new **jacke**t. A beautiful red one. It's online.

Sam: Is it cheap?

Jack: No, not really. But it's for Christmas!

Vocabulary

- to shop — faire du shopping
- to buy — acheter
- new — nouveau
- clothes — vêtements
- how often — à quelle fréquence
- once a month — une fois par mois
- expensive — cher
- cheap — bon marché
- online — en ligne
- trainers — baskets
- to wait — attendre
- till — jusqu'à
- Christmas — Noël
- jacket — veste

10A / 10b: Answer the questions

1. What is Katie's school uniform?
2. How often does Jack go shopping?
3. Does Jack want some new trainers for Christmas?

10C: What about you?

1. *Does your school have a uniform?*
2. *Do you like shopping?*
3. *What do you want for Christmas?*

LESSON 11

11A: Buying presents

Anna: It's almost Christmas!

Katie: Yes, it is. I want to buy my sister a **present**. But I don't know what to get her.

Anna: What does she want?

Katie: I don't know.

Anna: What does she like?

Katie: She likes clothes, music and animals.

Anna: Does she like dogs?

Katie: Yes, she loves them.

Anna: Why don't you get her a dog?

Katie: A dog? I really don't think my parents want a dog.

Anna: Okay. Maybe buy her a **dress** or a jacket.

Katie: They're too expensive. I don't have a lot of **money**.

Anna: Is it cold in Cambridge?

Katie: Yes, it's very cold.

Anna: What about a **hat**?

Katie: Good **idea**! Thanks!

Vocabulary
- present   cadeau
- dress   robe
- money   argent
- hat   chapeau
- idea   idée

11A: Fill the gaps

Anna:

Katie: Yes, it is. I want to buy my sister a present. But I don't know what to get her.

Anna:

Katie: I don't know.

Anna:

Katie: She likes clothes, music and animals.

Anna:

Katie: Yes, she loves them.

Anna:

Katie: A dog? I really don't think my parents want a dog.

Anna:

Katie: They're too expensive. I don't have a lot of money.

Anna:

Katie: Yes, it's very cold.

Anna:

Katie: Good idea! Thanks!

1. *Is it cold in Cambridge?*
2. *What about a hat?*
3. *Does she like dogs?*
4. *What does she like?*
5. *It's almost Christmas!*

6. *Okay. Maybe buy her a dress or a jacket.*
7. *What does she want?*
8. *Why don't you get her a dog?*

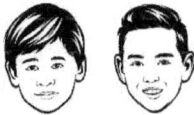

11B

Sam: Do you want to go to the Christmas **market,** Jack?

Jack: **Where** is it?

Sam: It's in the **city centre**.

Jack: Is it good?

Sam: Yes, it's great. There are nice **things** to **eat** and **drink**.

Jack: Can you buy Christmas presents there? I want to buy presents for my family.

Sam: Yes, there are lots of things to buy.

Jack: Is it expensive?

Sam: I think it's quite expensive. But if you like, we can go to the **shops** too.

Jack: Yes, that **sounds good**. When do you want to go?

Sam: How about Saturday **afternoon**?

Jack: Yes, Saturday's good. See you **then**.

Vocabulary
- market   marché
- city centre   centre ville
- thing   chose
- to eat   manger
- to drink   boire
- shop   magasin
- sounds good   ça sonne bien
- afternoon   après-midi
- then   à ce moment-là

11C: What about you?

1. *What does your mum want for Christmas?*
2. *Is it cheap or expensive?*

LESSON 12

12A: Christmas

Katie: What's Christmas like in France?

Anna: It's great. We get presents. We see all our family and eat lots of food!

Katie: We eat lots of food too, and **Father Christmas brings** us presents on **Christmas Day**.

Anna: Do you go to **church** at Christmas?

Katie: My family doesn't.

Anna: My school has a Christmas **party**. I love it!

Katie: At schools in the UK, there's **always** a Christmas **play**. All the little children are in the play.

Anna: I hope you have a good Christmas, Katie.

Katie: You too, Anna. **Merry Christmas**!

Vocabulary
- Father Christmas   Père Noël
- to bring   apporter
- Christmas Day   le jour de Noël
- church   l'église

- party   fête
- always   toujours
- play   pièce de théâtre
- Merry Christmas!   Joyeux Noël!

12B: What about you?

1. *What do you have to eat at Christmas?*
2. *Do you go to church at Christmas?*
3. *Does Father Christmas bring you presents?*

Word Search 2

```
Z D J H E P G R D L U N C H Z
I M Z K C D Z R J T Z J H N H
X C M P L B R C W Y P J E O I
J H O K T R A I N E R S A R N
V T E Q R L U C K Y F U P Q O
Y V A B O U T Z C Q Q N B K B
C R C H U R C H G C H N F Q A
V T P R S H B A L W A Y S E O
R A M D E A R L Y Y W J U N S
G W V Z R T M F Y H F X E P F
P D D V S M B W Q U V O Y P P
G D F H L O P Z U F V Z D S A
V H K C U W A U B W T Q B L B
H A D W S D Z P S A Q Q J Y Z
N Y E Q Y N D W U H O M E S G
```

- My school doesn't have a uniform. I wear **tr_in_rs** and **tr_us_rs** to school.
- Do you **a_w_ys** have **l_n_h** at school, or do you sometimes eat it at **h_m_**?
- You're **l_c_y**! You start school late. But I start school **_ar_y**.

- On Sunday, we go to  at **ab_ut h_lf** past ten.
- It sometimes rains in the summer. But it's often **s_n_y**.
- I want to buy a **_hea_** present for my friend, because I don't have a lot of money.

Réponses

Dialogue 2A: Find the right answer

1: a
2: b

Dialogue 4A: Find the right answer

1: b
2: c
3: c
4: c

Dialogue 6A: Find the right answer

1: c
2: b
3: b

Dialogue 8A Find the right answer

1: b
2: c
3: a

Dialogues 10A / 10B: Answer the questions

1. It's black trousers, a white shirt and a purple top.
2. He goes shopping about once a month.
3. No, he wants a new red jacket for Christmas.

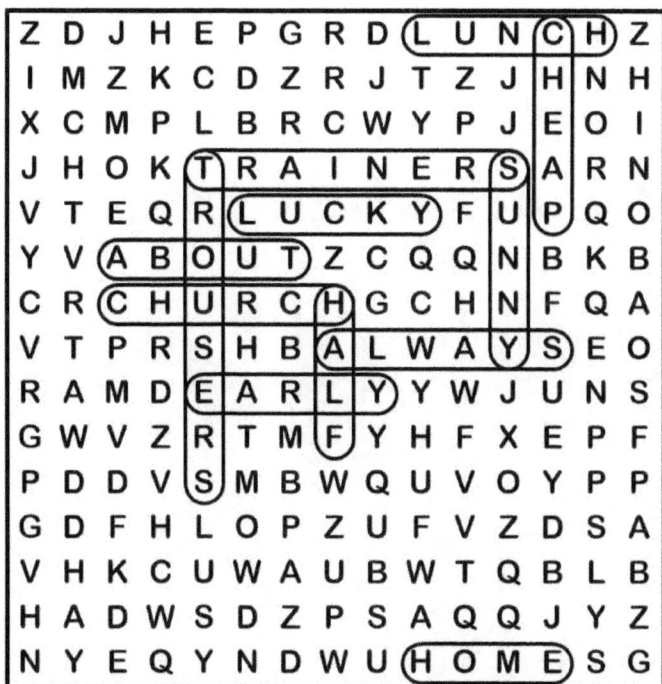

Merci d'avoir lu ce livre!

Si vous avez des questions ou des suggestions pour améliorer le livre, vous pouvez m'envoyer un courriel à l'adresse suivante: lydiawinter.zigzagenglish@gmail.com. Les suggestions pour de nouveaux livres sont toujours les bienvenues.

Vous trouverez le site web de Zigzag English ici: **www.zigzagenglish.co.uk**. Votre enfant et vous pouvez découvrir nos autres livres pour enfants et adultes, lire le blog et faire d'autres activités en anglais.

N'hésitez pas à laisser un avis pour ce livre. Merci beaucoup!

Dans les pages suivantes, vous trouverez des extraits d'autres livres destinés aux enfants de niveau débutant à élémentaire.

8A: A week's holiday

Katie: It's my **half term** holiday next week. A **whole** week with no school!

Anna: Are you going **away**?

Katie: Yes. We're going to the Lake District.

Anna: What's that? Where is it?

Katie: It's in the **north** of England. There are lots of **mountains** and **lakes**. It's very beautiful.

Anna: Lucky you! I have school next week.

Katie: School is really hard at the moment. I'm tired. I need a **break**.

Anna: Is your whole family going?

Katie: No. My mum has to work next week. So she's **staying** at home.

Anna: Your **poor** mum.

16. Too many boys and girls

Hi there! Is it your birthday today?

It's Poppy's birthday today. Poppy is nine today.

I don't like birthday parties. They're **noisy**. They're too noisy. There are lots of children. There are too many children.

Pam likes birthday parties. She likes noisy children. She likes eating birthday cake too.

I can't sit on my sofa. There are too many children in the living room! I can't eat my cat food. There are too many children in the kitchen! I can't look for a spider in the garden. That's **right** – there are too many boys and girls there!

Mum and Dad's bedroom is **quiet**. Their bed is quite comfortable.

See you tomorrow...

CHOOSE!

You can't always have everything you want.
Sometimes you have to choose.
So what do you choose?

- Ice cream or chocolate?
- A hamster or a rabbit?
- Homework or **housework**?
- A holiday at the beach or a skiing holiday?
- One very good friend or three good friends?
- Football or swimming?
- A green bedroom or a white bedroom?
- Autumn or spring?
- Chinese food or Italian food?
- Very hot **weather** or very cold weather?
- Orange juice or a milkshake?